ALL BEHIND YOU,
WINSTON

CHURCHILL'S GREAT COALITION 1940–45

ROGER HERMISTON

Aurum
Press

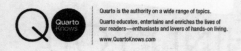

Quarto is the authority on a wide range of topics.
Quarto educates, entertains and enriches the lives of
our readers—enthusiasts and lovers of hands-on living.
www.QuartoKnows.com

First published in Great Britain in 2016
by Aurum Press Ltd, 74–77 White Lion Street, London N1 9PF

This paperback edition first published in 2017 by Aurum Press Ltd

A catalogue record for this book is available from the British Library.

ISBN 978 1 78131 664 1
ebook ISBN 978 1 78131 484 5

10 9 8 7 6 5 4 3 2
2021 2020 2019 2018 2017

Typeset by SX Composing DTP, Rayleigh, Essex
Printed and bound in Great Britain by CPI Group (UK) Ltd, Croydon, CR0 4YY

To Eileen, as always, and to Milton,
my constant companion during the writing of this book.

'This too, I know, that England does not love coalitions.'

Benjamin Disraeli, 16 December 1852

'We are trying to form a Government that should rally all the nation and set forth the energies of the people. I have not the slightest doubt about our victory, but I have no doubt at all as to the price that will have to be paid or the effort that will be needed.'

Clement Attlee, address to Labour Party conference,
morning of 13 May 1940

'Well, Ralph, what do I do next?'

Ernest Bevin to his Tory junior minister,
Ralph Assheton, on his first morning at the
Ministry of Labour, 14 May 1940